WALES
from the air

Photographs by
Simon Kirwan

Text by
Hilary Ellis

MYRIAD
LONDON

IRISH

SEA

Red Wharf
Bay
Amlwch
Benllech
Gt. Ormes
Head
Rhos-
on-Sea
Rhyl
Birkenhead
Liverpool
Holyhead
Anglesey
Llandudno
Kinmel Bay
Ellesmere Port
Beaumaris
Conwy
Colwyn Bay
Flint
Chester
Bangor
NT
Denbigh
Penrhyn Castle
Carnedd Llwelyn
Caernarfon
Tryfan
Ruthin
Wrexham
Llanberis
Glyders
SNOWDONIA
Caernarfon
Bay
Snowdon
Trefor
Nefyn
Porthmadog
Ffestiniog
Llyn Celyn
Corwen
Llangollen
Chirk
Criccieth
Portmeirion
Pwllheli
Oswestry
Abersoch
Tremadog
Bay
Harlech
Arenigs
Aberdaron
Mawddach
Estuary
Bardsey Island
Barmouth
Aran
Fawddwy
Shrewsbury
Cadair Idris
Dolgellau
Llyn Cau
Powis Castle
Welshpool
NT
Cardigan
Tywyn
Machynlleth
Montgomery
Aberdovey
Afon Dyfi
Newtown
Bay
Borth
Llanidloes
Aberystwyth
Ludlow
CAMBRIAN MOUNTAINS
Rhayader
R. Teme
New Quay
Llandrindod
Wells
Leominster
Cardigan
R. Teifi
Builth
Wells
Strumble Head
Hay-on-Wye
R. Wye
Fishguard
Llandovery
BLACK
MOUNTAINS
Hereford
St Davids
R. Usk
Brecon
St. Brides
Bay
Haverfordwest
Crickhowell
Milford
Haven
Carmarthen
BRECON
BEACONS
Abergavenny
Monmouth
Pembroke
Tenby
Laugharne
Raglan
Tintern Abbey
Carmarthen
Bay
Llanelli
Merthyr Tydfil
Ebbw
Vale
Chepstow
St. Govans Head
Swansea
Neath
Rhondda
Pontypridd
Caerphilly
Newport
Worms
Head
Oystermouth
Caswell Bay
Oxwich
Mumbles
Port Talbot
Avonmouth
Porthcawl
Llantrisant
Cardiff
Ogmore
Bristol
Barry

0 10 20 30 40 50 60 km
0 5 10 15 20 25 30 miles

Published in 2011 by Myriad Books Limited,
35 Bishopsthorpe Road, London SE26 4PA

Photographs copyright © Simon Kirwan
Text copyright © Hilary Ellis

Hilary Ellis has asserted her right under the
Copyright, Designs and Patents Act 1998 to be
identified as the author of this work.

ISBN 1 84746 014 3
EAN 978 1 84746 014 1

Designed by Jerry Goldie Graphic Design
Printed in China

www.myriadbooks.com

Title page: Moel Famau, the highest point in the
Clwydian Hills; opposite: dramatic Cwm Idwal,
cradled by the craggy peaks of the Glyders

Contents

Wales From the Air

What is it about the view from above that is so enthralling? I have always been fascinated by the vistas revealed from high places and soon discovered that mountain-walking satisfied this longing to look down from a high vantage point. Many of Britain's highest peaks are more than 3000 feet above sea-level and provide a lofty perch from which to view the surroundings.

The view from the air is different. The observer is no longer rooted to the ground but instead can soar above it, without the need to follow roads or footpaths. It is possible to take in wide areas at a glance and gain a far greater understanding of the relationships between the man-made and the natural landscape. From the ground, often only the largest features of the landscape – mountains, rivers, lakes and valleys – can be appreciated for their form and scale. From the air you can gain a much greater insight: a tidal estuary appears as an intricate network of channels, almost mirroring the roots of a tree; farmland often resembles a patchwork quilt; towns and cities, which may appear formless from the ground, can be seen to have grown around natural features, such as a river or surrounding hills.

Nowhere is this more true than in Wales, where the landscape has largely determined how the built environment has developed. In the north, the major settlements hug the coastline whether they are the coastal resorts of Llandudno and Prestatyn or the defensive towns of Conwy, Caernarfon and Beaumaris, guarded by the fortresses of Edward I's castles. Further inland the rocky cliffs and crags of Snowdonia safeguard the land from too much human encroachment. To the south, the Brecon Beacons mark the northern end of the industrial south. Today, little remains of the mining industry and the valleys that flow down to Cardiff are crammed with former coal and steel towns such as Merthyr Tydfil, Ebbw Vale and Pontypridd.

One of the many glories of Wales is its coastline and the best way to see it is from the air. The most westerly part of Wales along the Pembroke coast is marked by the rocky headland at St Davids and the windswept islands of Skokholm and Skomer just off the coast. The aerial viewpoint reveals the full drama of these remote outposts.

I have visited Wales many times over the years. When I look down on the familiar landscape from above I am reminded of the Welsh national anthem and the people who are fortunate to dwell in the country, "in which poets and minstrels rejoice".

Simon Kirwan

Left: Barmouth and the Mawddach estuary;
right: Crickhowell in its setting of the Brecon Beacons national park

THE NORTH COAST

While north Wales is mostly rural, a number of popular seaside resorts line the north coast from Rhyl to Pwllheli. Scattered among them are mighty medieval castles built by Edward I to subdue the Welsh. These castles, many of which are remarkably well preserved, dominate the estuaries, rivers and villages they stand alongside. The coast was once lined with small fishing villages but in the 19th century Victorians discovered the magnificent scenery and long, sandy beaches. The coastal resorts that developed attracted many visitors, particularly from the industrial towns of north-west England. They arrived first by paddle steamer, then by train. Though the land is relatively low-lying it is often backed dramatically by views of Snowdonia.

LLANDUDNO
The popular resort of Llandudno started life as a collection of fishermen's cottages. During the 19th century, the Mostyn family developed the town as a seaside resort on reclaimed marshland. The sweeping sands and long crescent promenade have attracted many tourists ever since and Llandudno is one of the most highly regarded of the North Wales beach resorts. The pier, on which as a youngster Ringo Starr of the Beatles worked, was once visited by paddle steamers from Liverpool. Now the pier provides entertainment for visitors including a permanent Punch and Judy show.

GREAT ORME & LITTLE ORME
Llandudno nestles between the two headlands of Great Orme and Little Orme. While the Great Orme rises to over 650ft (200m), Little Orme is just 463ft (141m) high. Known in Welsh as Rhiwledyn, Little Orme was inhabited during the Iron Age. A small hoard of Iron Age Celtic metalwork was found in a cave on the headland. The cliffs have been mined for limestone and are today popular with rock-climbers. A wildlife reserve is situated on Little Orme and the headland is a sanctuary for seabirds.

KINMEL BAY

Caravan parks and holiday camps cluster beside the long, wide sands at Kinmel Bay. Towyn and Kinmel Bay were developed close to the seaside resort of Rhyl in the 1920s on low-lying, former marshland next to the Irish Sea. The area was attractive to holiday-home buyers and those planning to retire, but in 1990 gale-force winds, a high tide and extreme wave conditions caused a breach in Towyn's sea defences. An area of 4sq m (6sq km) was flooded and thousands were evacuated. Sea defences have since been strengthened.

POINT OF AYR *left*

At the north-west corner of the Dee estuary is the 18th century Point of Ayr lighthouse (also called Talacre). The lighthouse has been been out of action since 1883 and can be reached by foot at low tide from Talacre Beach. The beach has fantastic views out to the Irish Sea and is a popular spot with birdwatchers. The region is often the first landfall for birds crossing over from the north-west coast of England.

RHOS-ON-SEA *above*

The seaside resort of Rhos-on-Sea (Llandrillo-yn-Rhos) is one mile north of Colwyn Bay. A plaque on the seafront records the legend that the Welsh prince, Madoc ap Owain Gwynedd, sailed from Rhos in 1170 and discovered America 300 years before Christopher Columbus. The town is famous for its sixth-century church, St Trillo's Chapel, built on the site of a pre-Christian holy well. It is the smallest chapel in Britain and seats just six people. The chapel stands on the foreshore, protected by an extended promenade and sea wall.

RHYL *left*

The Foryd Bridge, known popularly as the blue bridge, is one of the great landmarks of Rhyl and a gateway to the seaside resort. Rhyl's extensive sands have long been popular with holidaymakers. Crowds flock to the promenade and Marine Lake Pleasure Beach for family fun and amusements.

GREAT ORME

The massive limestone headland of Great Orme rises to over 650ft (200m) and dominates the resort of Llandudno and its two beaches. Prehistoric sites on Great Orme include stone circles, burial sites and the remains of Bronze Age copper mines. Mining continued in the 17th century and the mines, once open-cast, then dug into the landscape, are now open to the public. The mining museum exhibits some of the Paleolithic and Bronze Age artefacts found on the headland. Sheep and feral goats graze Great Orme enjoying the milder climate. The headland is famous for its butterfly population and there are spectacular views from Great Orme's Head out to Puffin Island and the Irish Sea. It is thought that the name Orme derives from an old Norse word for sea monster, which is how the headland might have appeared to sailors as it loomed up out of the sea mists. The summit and country park can be reached by the Great Orme tramway, built in 1902 and Britain's only cable hauled, public road tramway.

RUTHIN *above*

The market town of Ruthin is the site of a baronial castle known as the Red Fort. Built by Edward I in the late 13th century, today all that remains are three towers and a ruined gatehouse. This once formidable castle with five round towers was burnt in attacks by Owain Glyndŵr in the early 15th century, and beseiged during the Civil War. In 1646 the castle was destroyed by order of Parliament. The town has a population of around 5,000 and lies at the end of the Vale of Clwyd. Like the castle, much of the town is built in red sandstone; the name Ruthin in Welsh comes from *rhudd* meaning red and *din* meaning a city. All of the streets in the centre of the town head uphill to St Peter's Square, from where there are good views of the surrounding countryside.

CORWEN *right*

Situated in a central location in the Dee Valley, Corwen is known as the Crossroads of North Wales. In Victorian times, the market town was a popular stopping place on the main road from London to Holyhead and for centuries provided an overnight stop for cattle-drovers. Corwen is a busy town, packed with hotels which developed to serve the stagecoach route to Holyhead. The town is associated with the Welsh hero, Owain Glyndŵr, who used the town as a base. Nearby is Caer Drewyn, the mountain where Glyndŵr stopped to rest his army before marching on to Ruthin. From the top there are good views of the town. A modern sculpture in Corwen town square commemorates Glyndŵr's revolt against Henry IV in the 15th century.

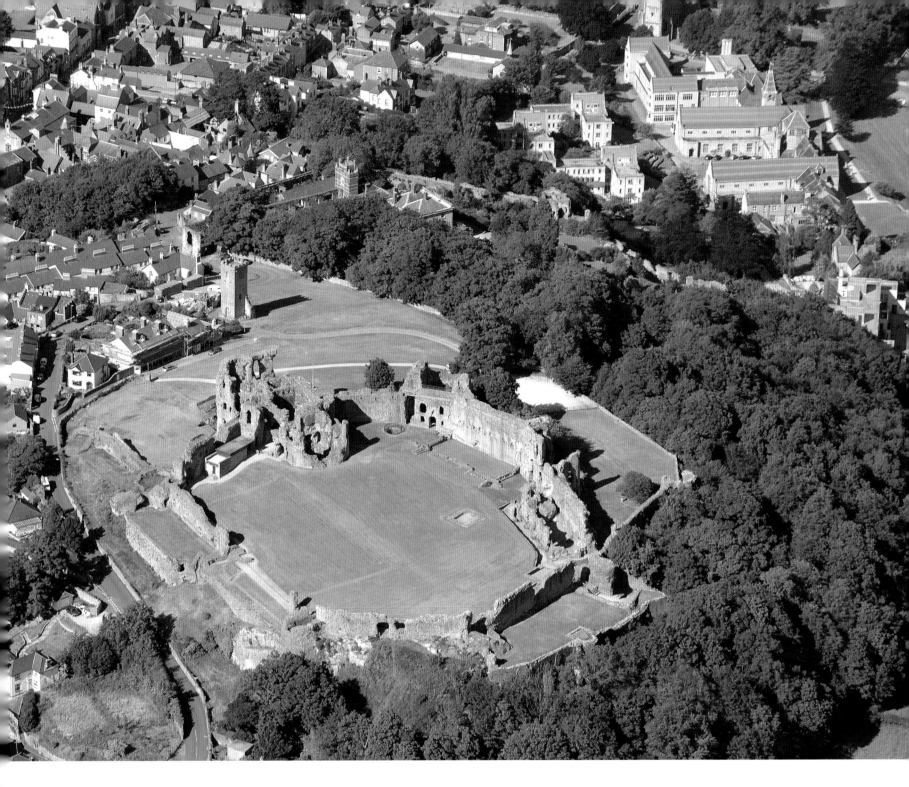

DENBIGH *above*

The ruins of Edward I's 13th-century castle overlook the historic market town of Denbigh. Designed by Edward's architect, Master James of St George, the castle was built on the site of an earlier Welsh fortress. In the 11th century Denbigh was a residence of Welsh princes. Edward conquered the town and granted the territory to Henry de Lacy, the Earl of Lincoln, and work began on a castle. Its great triple-towered gatehouse can be seen at the north side of the castle walls in this photograph. The castle was originally planned on a grander scale and the curtain walls became town walls that can still be seen today.

GLAN CONWY

Between Llanrwst and Llandudno, the river Conwy (Afon Conwy) winds its way through fertile and picturesque surroundings. The A470 follows the route, as does a railway on the Conwy Valley Line that travels from Blaenau Ffestiniog through to Conwy. Built in the Victorian era, the railway was designed to carry slate to port at Deganwy. During spring tides, the river is tidal as far as Llanrwst (approximately 12 miles inland) and the land is suitable for dairy farming and sheep rearing. In the coldest period of winter, sheep are brought down from Snowdonia's mountains for the valley's less harsh conditions. The Romans occupied this area up to 400AD and the site of Canovium Roman Fort can be seen beside the river close to Tanrallt. To the west among the craggy hills, Bodnant Garden overlooks the valley near its mouth. Containing over 80 acres of gardens surrounding Bodnant Hall, this impressive location is popular with both amateur and professional gardeners for its wide range of foliage.

CONWY

The small, walled town of Conwy lies south of Llandudno, Deganwy and the Great Orme headland. Edward I's dark-stoned medieval castle dominates the estuary and is met by three parallel bridges. Robert Stephenson's tubular railway bridge is furthest from the sea and was designed with mock fortifications at each end. Two further bridges for road traffic include a suspension bridge designed by Thomas Telford and a road bridge. Conwy was once on the main route to Holyhead but today most traffic passes through an immersed tube tunnel under the estuary. The town is popular with day-trippers and

the castle is its main attraction. Construction began in 1283 and was completed within four years. A key fortress in Edward's fearsome "iron ring" of castles built to subdue the Welsh, the castle relies on a simple design and a prominent location. The town walls were built at the same time and these can still be seen today. Other attractions include a fisherman's cottage, said to be the smallest house in Britain, a beautiful quay, and plenty of tea and coffee shops. Conwy was founded when Llywelyn the Great founded the Abbey of Aberconwy in the 13th century. His statue graces Conwy's main square.

BANGOR

A monastic community was founded here in the sixth century and the town's name is derived from the wattle fence that surrounded the monks' enclosure – *bangori*. Bangor's cathedral dates from the 13th century and was the burial site of the Welsh prince, Owain Gwynedd. During the middle ages, his tomb was the starting point for pilgrimages to Bardsey Island. The city's population quadrupled in the early 19th century with the slate boom and many passengers began to arrive by railway. The Victoria pier, built in 1896, now beautifully restored, can be seen at the tip of the Menai Strait. Before the Menai Bridge was built, boats would set off to Anglesey from the pier, which is now listed. Today Bangor is famous for its university, which opened in 1884 in an old coaching inn with 58 students. The university moved to the hillside overlooking Bangor in 1911 and now has over 8,000 students – a substantial proportion of Bangor's 12,000 residents.

PUFFIN ISLAND

Often called *Ynys Seriol*, Puffin Island is the home of St Seriol's sanctuary and is situated at the tip of Anglesey. The remains of monastic buildings that date back to the sixth century can be seen across the island. Once known as Priestholm, the island probably gained its new name due to the large number of puffins that colonised the rocky cliffs. At one time up to 2,000 pairs were recorded. The number of puffins declined rapidly after brown rats were accidentally introduced to the island. A programme of rat poisoning in 1998 has seen the puffin population increase again.

PENRHYN CASTLE

West of Bangor lies Penrhyn Castle, a dramatic 19th-century castle and garden now owned by the National Trust. The building was the home of the Pennant family, who made their fortune through sugar estates in Jamaica and from the nearby slate trade. The mock castle has a Norman-style exterior and opulent interiors in a range of styles. Though a stone castle was built on the site in the 15th century, most of today's building was completed in the 19th century to designs by Thomas Hopper. The attractive gardens that surround the castle include a Victorian walled garden, extensive informal gardens, a dolls' museum, an industrial railway museum, a model railway museum and an adventure playground.

BEAUMARIS

The castle at Beaumaris was the last and largest of the castles built by Edward I to restrain the Welsh. Designed by Edward's favourite architect, Master James of St George, Beaumaris is a true concentric castle with almost geometric symmetry. It saw little action apart from during the Civil War and the building was never fully completed. The picturesque 13th-century town that grew up around the castle has a Victorian gaol and courthouse. Today it is packed with brightly coloured antique shops and lively pubs, cafés and restaurants. Until the 1950s, paddle steamers from Liverpool brought thousands of tourists to Beaumaris pier on their way down the Menai Strait to Caernarfon. Beaumaris was known as Rhosfair and Barnover, but named Beaumaris by Edward I from the French for "beautiful marsh". The castle itself was erected on low ground so that vessels might unload under its walls.

MENAI BRIDGES

The north Wales mainland and the Isle of Anglesey are separated by the Menai Strait, bridged first in 1826 by Thomas Telford. It was just one of the many challenges faced by Telford in improving the London to Holyhead road, essential for crossings to Ireland. His Menai suspension bridge (right) replaced a treacherous ferry journey from Bangor across the tidal strait. Many boats capsized or ran aground, and 54 people were swept away by a high tide in 1785 after their boat became stranded on a sandbar. Telford proposed a suspension bridge far larger than any previously built, to allow tall sailing ships to continue along the Strait. Robert Stephenson's tubular bridge followed in 1850. After a disastrous fire in 1970, the bridge was reconstructed to carry both trains and road traffic. The view above shows Stephenson's bridge, followed by Telford's, and views beyond to the Lavan Sands and the Irish Sea.

Benllech

The popular seaside resort of Benllech is famous for its fine golden sands and clear blue water. Set in a crescent-shaped bay and surrounded by fossil-studded cliffs, the low tide reveals miles of beautiful beach but strong tidal currents can be a hazard. The area is rich in ancient history: a neolithic burial chamber and the remains of 4th-century huts are close by, whilst the grave of a Viking was found in 1945 on a sandy ridge facing Benllech Sands. Coins have been found here suggesting Romans occupied the area.

RED WHARF BAY

On the east coast of Anglesey, Red Wharf Bay or Traeth Coch is the largest beach on the island at low tide. At high tide, making your way around the beach involves a lengthy five-mile walk across muddy saltmarsh shores and sand dunes. The bay has several small rock pools and attracts a large number of waterfowl and wading birds, including curlew, oystercatchers, purple sandpipers and grey plover.

CAERNARFON CASTLE

Positioned on a peninsula at the foot of the Menai Strait, Caernarfon Castle is a mighty presence standing on the site of previous Norman and Roman fortifications. One of Edward I's many military strongholds, its polygonal towers and curtain walls were inspired by the Roman city of Constantinople. The Eagle Tower, closest to the Strait, was crowned with stone eagles as a symbol of imperial power. Edward's son was born in the castle and became the first English Prince of Wales in 1301. In the 20th century, both Edward VIII and Prince Charles became Princes of Wales in controversial investiture ceremonies held in the castle.

SNOWDONIA

The name Snowdonia derives from the Gaelic *Snaudune*, meaning Snowy Hills. Sailors travelling on ships from Ireland in the dark ages called the snow-covered peaks by this name. Snowdonia's main peaks were also known by the Welsh as *Yr Eryri*, meaning "the abode of the eagles". Stretching from the sea at Conwy in the north to Aberdyfi beyond Cadair Idris in the south, Snowdonia covers some 838sq miles (2170sq km). The national park, founded in 1951, was the first to be designated in Wales. Its spectacular peaks and vistas bring millions of visitors to Snowdonia each year. There are more than 90 summits over 2,000ft and 15 over 3,000ft. The highest mountain, Snowdon (*Yr Wyddfa*) at 3560ft (1085m), dominates northern Snowdonia. In southern Snowdonia the two highest peaks are Aran Fawddwy at 2970ft (905m) and Penygadair at 2929ft (893m) on Cadair Idris.

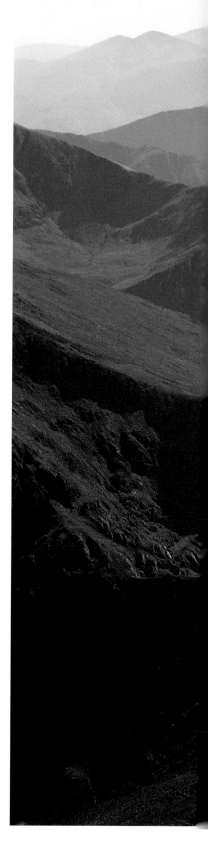

CARNEDD LLYWELYN

Carnedd Llywelyn is the highest peak in the Carneddau range at 3491ft (1064m) and the second highest in Wales. There are several peaks in the range over 2500ft (760m) high, making it the largest continuous area of high ground in Wales. Carnedd Llywelyn can be approached by a number of routes, all of them long, and the range extends as far north as the Conwy valley. The summit is flat and boulder-strewn, but the cliffs surrounding the summit are famous for rock climbs, including Ysgolion Duon (meaning "black ladders"). The mountain's name translates as "Llywelyn's cairn" and refers to one of the two Welsh princes of the 13th century, Llywelyn the Great and his grandson Llywelyn ap Gruffydd.

TRYFAN & CWM IDWAL

The giant buttresses of Tryfan ("the Trident"), including Milestone Buttress, were among the first crags to attract rock climbers. Some of the most challenging climbs and scrambles in Snowdonia are found among the peaks in this range. In the 1950s the team who led the first successful Everest expedition trained on these peaks. Nearby Cwm Idwal is arguably the most dramatic cwm in North Wales. Cradled by the three craggy peaks of Glyder Fawr, Twll Du and Y Garn, the cwm is a nature reserve with unusually rich plant life. Legend has it that a moraine on the lake's western shore is the burial place of the giant, Idwal and it is also believed that no bird flies over the lake's surface.

CARNEDD LLYWELYN

This photograph shows some of North Snowdonia's typically rugged mountain scenery and gives a taste of the long hikes and dangerous climbs, as well as the fantastic and rewarding views. The photograph looks to the south-east and takes in Carnedd Llywelyn and the low slopes of Carnedd Moel Siabod beyond.

LLYN OGWEN

Almost 990ft (300m) above sea level, Llyn Ogwen is one of the shallowest lakes in the area at an average of just 6ft (1.8m) deep. Yet trout thrive in its light blue waters. Around the lake, along a fisherman's path, are views of Tryfan's giant buttresses.

GLYDER FACH & FAWR

The Glyders – Glyder Fach and Glyder Fawr – are challenging hikes that offer breathtaking views of Snowdon across the Llanberis Pass. To the north-west lies Anglesey, beyond the Menai Strait. This view takes in the lakes beside Llanberis, Llyn Peris and Llyn Padarn. The Afon Rhythallt flows from the lakes, becomes the Afon Seiont and meets the sea at Caernarfon.

GLYDER FACH SUMMIT *below*

An enormous collection of slabs and boulders marks the summit of Glyder Fach. Reaching the summit from Bwlch Tryfan can involve a good scramble up the Bristly Ridge. The route passes an over-hanging "cantilever" rock, settled on a prominent pile of rocks.

LLANBERIS PASS

The Afon Nant Peris runs along the length of the rugged Llanberis Pass carrying the main A4086 road from Llanberis over Pen-y-Pass between the mountain ranges of the Glyderau and the Snowdon massif. This road was built in the early 19th century by local mining companies, and sheep straddle the narrow road that is almost blocked by large boulders and stones. Climbers flock to Pen-y-Pass, the highest starting point for hikes to the Snowdon Horseshoe.

CRIB GOCH & SNOWDON

Snowdon's summit, known as Yr Wyddfa, is the highest point in Wales at 3560ft (1085m). Three popular hikes lead to the top, one of which follows the ridge of Crib Goch, seen here before the lake. This sharp ridge joins Snowdon, Crib Goch and Y Lliwedd and is known as the Snowdon Horseshoe. Moel Hebog at 2566ft (782m) can be seen among the clouds.

Y LLIWEDD & SNOWDON

This alternative view of the Snowdon Horseshoe shows Y Lliwedd in the foreground, the small corrie lake of Llyn Llydaw and, further down, Llyn Teyrn. Many Arthurian legends are associated with locations around Snowdon, and *Teyrn*, meaning monarch, most probably refers to King Arthur. Llyn Llydaw is the Welsh claimant to the home of the Lady of the Lake.

SNOWDON

Snowdon is famous as the most climbed mountain in Britain, with thousands reaching the summit each week. Most follow the least daunting route, the Llanberis Track, also known as the Tourist Path. Another ascent follows the Miner's Track, used when copper mines were sited high in the mountains. The summit can also be reached by the Snowdon Mountain Railway, a five mile (8km) scenic route from nearby Llanberis. A great triumph of Victorian engineering, the railway opened in 1896 and is the only rack and pinion railway in Britain. It passes a waterfall and disused mines, and from the final station there is a short walk to the summit. Before the railway was completed, the less active were carried to the summit by ponies. Despite the large numbers who climb Snowdon, it is not an easy ascent. The weather can change dramatically and walkers must always be prepared.

LLYN CELYN

At the foot of the Arenig mountains lies Llyn Celyn, a fine lake over two miles in length. The lake is actually a reservoir, created to control the flow of the river Dee and provide water for Liverpool. Despite vigorous local opposition, the marshy Tryweryn valley was flooded in 1965, along with the old Welsh-speaking village of Capel Celyn. A lakeside chapel commemorates the community and those buried in its drowned graveyard. Also found here is a memorial stone dedicated to a group of local Quakers who emigrated to America to escape persecution.

ARENIG FAWR

Arenig Fawr towers over Llyn Arenig Fawr and the surrounding barren moorland. Standing 2800ft (854m) high, the summit has spectacular views across the edge of Snowdonia and Bala lake. A Flying Fortress crashed here in 1943 when the mountain was shrouded in cloud, killing the entire crew. A memorial stone can be found on the summit dedicated to their memory. George Borrow, during his journey through Wales in 1854, described the mountain as majestic. Of all the hills he saw, Arenig Fawr made the greatest impression.

RHINOGS & MOEL-Y-GEST

The rugged Rhinog mountains overlook many of the coastal villages of west Snowdonia. Geologically ancient, the volcanic rock in this region was carved into distinctive escarpments by thick glaciers during the last Ice Age. Drovers led packhorses through the passes along ancient routes, while bandits who raided lands to the east hid among the hills. Feral goats roam the valleys, while buzzards and cuckoos can be spotted overhead. On the route to Rhinog Fawr lie the Roman Steps, a series of slabs laid down in medieval times by drovers. The route

was used in prehistoric times and by the Romans, who may have improved the surface.

Moel-y-Gest, at 859ft (262m) is a small mountain above the town of Porthmadog. The climb to the summit is not too strenuous and gives impressive views of many peaks in the region. The mountain's craggy rocks are distinctive and overlook Borth-y-Gest, at the gateway to the Lleyn peninsula. Rock climbers use this miniature mountain to practise their skills when the mountains of Snowdonia are not accessible due to snow or bad weather.

ARAN FAWDDWY

Crowning the highest ridge of southern Snowdonia, Aran Fawddwy reaches 2976ft (905m). The summit's stony cairn is said to have been erected by the men of Dinas Mawddwy when they believed Cadair Idris to be 6ft (2m) higher. In fact, Aran Fawddwy is 43ft (13m) higher. Both Aran Fawddwy and Aran Benllyn, a mile along the ridge, are associated with Arthurian legends. King Arthur is said to have fought a mighty battle nearby with a giant, Rhita Gawr, who lived on the southern edge of Aran Fawddwy. The giant wished to make a collar for his robe from Arthur's beard. Arthur fought the giant and won, flinging him down the hillside. Aran Benllyn is one of the many places the giant is said to have been buried.

TYRRAU MAWR

On the west side of Cadair Idris lies the foreboding and heather-clad flank of Tyrrau Mawr. Known also as Craig-las, the craggy hill reaches 2168ft (661m). Views from Barmouth in the north-west are dominated by its looming bulk. One route to Cadair Idris's peak follows the ridge walk along the top of this mountain. It is a good hour's walk from Tyrrau Mawr along the Pony Path beyond to the summit at Penygadair. The route was probably used by the Victorians who visited the mountain and hired ponies as guides. It may have also been used by packhorses in medieval times. Tyrrau Mawr overlooks the eerie Cregennen Lakes and the spectacular Mawddach Estuary. Beyond the Afon Mawddach, views stretch across to Barmouth and the remote Lleyn peninsula. Cadair Idris and its surroundings are a national nature reserve and one of the most southern habitats of Britain for arctic alpine plants.

CREGENNEN LAKES

In a haunting spot below Tyrrau Mawr, among small boulders and reeds, lie the crystal clear blue waters of the Llynau Cregennen. These two magical lakes are situated over 750ft (230m) above the Mawddach Estuary in a green and undulating plateau landscape.

LLYN CAU

Llyn Cau is an almost ideal location for a high mountain lake:
flanked to the south by the pointed crag of Craig Cau and to
the north by the imposing ridge of Cadair Idris and its peaks.
The 18th-century artist Richard Wilson, who inspired many
including Turner, painted a magnificent composition of the
lake with an exaggerated precipice and invented features. The
lake is a fine example of a glaciated cwm with corries, steep
eroded sides and morainic debris at the lake's outflow.

LLYN Y GADAIR

The hollow corrie lake of Llyn Y Gadair is one of a handful
surrounding the summit of Cadair Idris. It lies to the north
of Penygadair and the Pony Path that heads to the rocky cliffs
of Cyfrwy (The Saddle). It's a sheer drop from the path down
to the magnificent lake. This view looks southward, beyond
the peaks of Cadair Idris and the ridge of the Minfford Path
to Craig Goch on the south side of Tal-y-llyn Lake.

CADAIR IDRIS

At 2929ft (893m), the summit of Cadair Idris – Penygadair – is not the highest peak in southern Snowdonia, but its open access offers exceptional views. On a very clear day, Bardsey Island can be seen, 40 miles (65 km) away at the tip of the Lleyn peninsula. Cadair Idris means the chair of Idris, and Penygadair refers to the top of the chair. Idris may have been Idris Gawr, a legendary Celtic poet and giant who liked to study the stars from his high throne. In one popular story, though it is not a tale exclusive to this mountain, a visitor who spends a night alone on the summit will return either as a madman or a poet. A number of named paths lead to the summit including the Pony Path, the Minfford Path and the Fox's Path. The latter is now a dangerous descent due to erosion on the pathway.

CADAIR IDRIS

Summits along the northern flank of Cadair Idris have dramatic cliffs and steep drops. Llyn y Gadair is seen here cradled by the peaks of Penygadair and Cyfrwy (the Saddle), and the adjoining ridge that climbers follow on the Pony Path. The ridge continues to Mynydd Moel, still over 2830ft (863m) high. The cliffs are particularly dangerous at Cyfrwy, seen in the foreground of this photograph. Llyn Gafr can be seen further down the mountain, among the heather-clad rocky slopes. Cadair Idris is situated close to Dolgellau at the southern end of Snowdonia and the low slopes and valleys can be seen in the distance. When the Victorians discovered the Welsh mountains, Cadair Idris became a popular climb for many tourists on hired ponies with guides. An old lady trekked early each morning to the summit hut to serve cups of tea to those who managed the climb.

NORTH-WEST COAST

This beautifully scenic region stretches from the remote coves and rocky headlands of the Lleyn peninsula to the magnificent estuaries and sandy beaches of Snowdonia's western coastline. Increasingly popular with holidaymakers seeking surf and sail, the region was once home to a number of busy ports where shipbuilding and the export of coal meant Snowdonia was known around the world. The Lleyn peninsula is the Land's End of north Wales, and has been a place of pilgrimage for centuries. Thousands of saints made the journey to Bardsey Island at the peninsula's tip, travelling by boat across the treacherous Bardsey Sound. The coastline is home to a number of rare birds including the chough, which nests on the peninsula. Migrating birds and wildlife flock to the mudflats of the Glaslyn and Mawddach rivers. These picturesque estuaries have inspired artists and writers over the centuries.

TREFOR

The coastal village of Trefor lies on the north side of the Lleyn peninsula. Two ancient-looking hills, Gurn Ddu and Moel-Pen-llechog, are seen here overlooking the road between Trefor and Clynnog Fawr to the north-east. The hills appear to sweep down to the sand and shingle beach. On a clear day it is possible to see the coast of Ireland and the Wicklow Mountains across the Irish Sea. A large colony of seals inhabits this stretch of coastline.

YR EIFL

Trefor is overlooked to the south-east by the steep mountain of Yr Eifl (The Rivals), whose summit reaches 1850ft (560m). From the top are stunning views of Caernarfon Bay, Anglesey and across the Lleyn peninsula. The mountain sides have been quarried in the past and Trefor was once a bustling port exporting granite around the world. On the slopes of the hill is Tre'r Ceiri (Town of the Giants), a spectacular Iron Age fort of 150 huts surrounded by a stone wall.

NEFYN

The small town of Nefyn lies on the north-west coast of the Lleyn peninsula overlooking Caernarfon Bay. It is at the southern end of a long sandy bay, beside the headland in the centre of this sweeping scene (above). It was once on the Pilgrim's Route to Bardsey Island and relics from this time can be seen at the church of St Mary, along with exhibits from Nefyn's maritime past.

In 1284 when Edward I celebrated his conquest over Wales with a tournament in Nefyn it was still a small fishing village, but an important place for trade. There has been herring fishing in Nefyn since the 13th century, and a major proportion of the village's male population fished the seas in the 17th, 18th and 19th centuries. Nefyn is now a quiet holiday destination in the heart of a Welsh-speaking community.

PORTH DINLLAEN *right*

Close to Nefyn, the pretty village of Porth Dinllaen can be reached by walking west towards the end of the promontory along the beach. Alternatively there is a car park at Morfa Nefyn close to the golf course. The natural harbour at Porth Dinllaen was considered for development as the main port for ferries to Ireland, but instead this role fell to Holyhead. The long, curving bay is backed by low cliffs. To the western end are clustered the fishing cottages of the tiny 18th-century Porth Dinllaen hamlet now owned by the National Trust. The Trust acquired the property in 1984 and it consists of 16 houses, the lifeboat station and the Ty Coch Inn. The beach is a perfect place for picnics, walks and bathing; the red-painted inn is an ideal stop for a drink and a bite to eat. Seals can often be seen on the rocks at the western promontory.

PARWYD

The cove of Parwyd is a fantastic site for geology as the lines and folds of volcanic deposits can be clearly seen; these rocks were deposited some 500 million years ago. Though boulder and rock climbing is popular, the rock here is not solid. Situated on the southern tip of the Lleyn peninsula, the cove faces Bardsey Island across the sound, and the tiny island rock of Carreg Ddu is also close. The coastline here is maintained by the National Trust and feels like the end of the earth. Prehistoric stone blades have been found in the area.

PORTH IAGO *right*

This remote, south-west facing cove is on the Caernarfon Bay side of the Lleyn peninsula. The sheltered aspect and golden sands make this a peaceful spot for families. The beach is small and unspoilt with steep cliffs surrounding the narrow inlet. The promontory is also a good site for fishing, which can be done at the discretion of the local farmer at Ty Mawr, and produces bass, wrasse and pollack. A number of shipwrecks are found in this area, as many ships have succumbed to the strong winds and ragged rocks of the peninsula.

PORTH COLMON

This quiet village lies at the southern end of the wide and sandy Traeth Penllech beach on the northern side of the Lleyn peninsula, south-west of Nefyn. Small boats can be launched from the harbour, and lobster and crab are locally available. The beach is popular with surfers during the winter and spring, though strong rip tides can make conditions hazardous. Porth Colmon's sandy coves are attractive and secluded for all the family in fine weather.

BARDSEY ISLAND

Just off the tip of the Lleyn peninsula lies Bardsey Island, a site of pilgrimage for Christians through the ages. So many Christian pilgrims sought sanctuary and were buried on the island that it became known as the Isle of 20,000 Saints. Settlement of the island is thought to have begun in the Dark Ages, but the death of St Dyfrig on the island marked the start of the pilgrimages. Remains of the graves of pilgrims can be seen across the island. Bardsey Island, also known as Ynys Enlli, is now a seabird sanctuary and wildlife refuge. The island is dominated by a large hill, Mynydd Enlli, which reaches a height of 548ft (167m). Since the 18th century, a fishing and farming community has become established on the island and today the majority of the land is still farmed. A lighthouse can be seen clearly on the low-lying land to the island's south-west side. Built in 1821, it is the tallest square-towered lighthouse in the UK at 99ft (30m). It was automated in 1987.

UWCHMYNYDD

The last headland at the end of the Lleyn peninsula, generally referred to as Uwchmynydd, is the Land's End of north Wales. To get there, walkers pass over open grassland criss-crossed with sheep tracks and scattered with small fields, sheep and heather. The headland's summit, Mynydd Mawr, seen to the left of this photograph, is a wild and enchanting spot. From the hillside are magnificent views across the Bardsey Sound, a two-mile stretch of water with dangerous tides and currents, to Bardsey Island. In fact, Bardsey Island's Welsh name, Ynys Enlli, means Island of the Currents. The coastal heath is an important feeding ground for the rare chough, while buzzards and hawks can be spotted among the sea birds. The remote coves that surround the headland were used by early pilgrims as departure points on their route to Bardsey Island. The ruins of the church where saints waited to cross the Sound can still be seen.

ABERSOCH

On the south side of the Lleyn peninsula, Abersoch is known throughout Wales and beyond for its yachting and sailing. The natural harbour and sandbanks stretch for two to three miles into Tremadog Bay, and the flat waters are ideal for watersports enthusiasts. The town is crowded at peak season and its three beaches are full of activity. The main beach is always busy with international events and national championships. They range from extreme sports such as wakeboarding and Zapcat racing to longboat challenges, dinghy racing and regattas.

ABERDARON *left*

The whitewashed cottages of Aberdaron cluster beside the wide sand and shingle bay. Pilgrims on their way to Ynys Enlli would depart from this remote fishing village, stopping for food and shelter at the 14th-century Y-Gegin Fawr ("the Old Kitchen"). Day visits to the island can still be arranged, setting sail from Aberdaron. The Church of St Hywyn in the village was built in the 12th century by Gruffydd ap Cynan, King of Gwynedd, and enlarged in 1417. The stone buildings replaced wooden structures, which had been used for worship since the 5th century. This is a sanctuary church where disputes can be settled on the stone chair of peace, and no fugitive can be ejected for 40 days and nights. The beach at Aberdaron can be busy in summer with surfing and sailing enthusiasts. Annual events bring hundreds of visitors to the beach and include a regatta with races for all levels and a festival with concerts and competitions.

PWLLHELI

Hundreds of yachts are berthed in the large marina at Pwllheli, the unofficial capital and market town of the Lleyn peninsula. Pwllheli means saltwater pool and the harbour has always played an important role for the town. Pwllheli was a centre for shipbuilding and sea trade for many years and wine was imported from the continent. Today the harbour is almost landlocked due to the gradual build-up of sand and the decline of sea trading in the area. Pwllheli was reinvented as a holiday town. The railway brought tourists from industrial areas to Pwllheli's two sandy beaches and recreational spots including a seafront promenade and Butlin's holiday camp. A mile up a country road from the holiday camp, now run by Haven, is the 15th-century manor house, Penarth Fawr. Built with local stones and timber and including many original features, the house provides a unique example of how the Welsh gentry lived at the time.

CRICCIETH *above*

The castle at Criccieth stands high on an outcrop of green felsite rock on the northern shores of Cardigan Bay. Reached by a steep climb, the castle was originally built by Llywelyn the Great as a stronghold of the Welsh princes but changed hands several times and was finally ruined by fire. It has now been restored and an on-site museum explains its history. The romantic ruins have inspired many artists and there are fine views down to the Lleyn peninsula and north-east towards Snowdonia. Criccieth's two beaches, with safe swimming and bathing, attract frequent visits from porpoises. Criccieth is known as "the pearl of Wales on the shore of Snowdonia" and is a pleasant family resort. It is most famous for its associations with David Lloyd George, the Liberal statesman and prime minister who grew up nearby and established his own law practice in the town. Lloyd George gained a reputation as a solicitor willing to defend people against those in authority. Elected as a member of parliament at the age of 27, his famously fiery speeches attracted huge audiences at political meetings in Market Square.

PORTHMADOG
right & below

In the early 19th century, an English MP and local landowner named William Alexander Madocks decided to develop a town and port where travellers could stop off on their way to Ireland. At the time, Porth Dinllaen on the Lleyn peninsula was expected to become the major port, rather than Holyhead on Anglesey. Madocks built a sea wall and embankment across the Glaslyn Estuary, draining and reclaiming marshy land. He planned two towns: Tremadog and Porthmadog. The latter prospered as a port with the successful export of slate around the world.

PORTHMADOG

The mile-long embankment across the Glaslyn Estuary, the Cob, was built in a spectacular spot, just south of the Moelwyns and Cnicht. Before its construction, the estuary was said to be the most beautiful in the whole of Wales. Today, it is a haven for migrating birds and wildlife. Completed in 1811, the embankment reclaimed over 7,000 acres of land from the river's mudflats. Tourists can take the Ffestiniog railway from the harbour, along the Cob and into the mountains as far as Blaenau Ffestiniog. The steam railway was originally built to carry slate from the mines of Snowdonia to the harbour for shipping.

PORTMEIRION *right*

Built by the architect Sir Clough Williams-Ellis between 1925 and 1975, Portmeirion is an Italianate coastal village of eclectic buildings, many salvaged from demolition sites. Surrounded by sub-tropical gardens and woodlands, Portmeirion is a hotel and holiday village that has inspired guests and visitors such as Noel Coward, who wrote the play *Blythe Spirit* here in 1941. Patrick McGoohan used Portmeirion as a location for his enigmatic Sixties television series, *The Prisoner*. The wide sands of the Traeth Bach Estuary lie in front of the village, with the mountains of Meirionnydd as a backdrop.

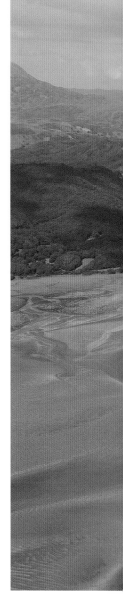

BARMOUTH

Close to Cadair Idris, and at the foot of the Mawddach Estuary, Barmouth is best known today for its tourism. But during the middle ages, Barmouth was a bustling port known as Aber Mawddach, often shortened to Abermaw. In the oldest part of town, attractive houses nestle on the steep streets and terraces of Dinas Oleu hill, the first property ever donated to the National Trust. Another visitor attraction is Barmouth Bridge, now crossed by trains on the Cambrian Coast Line. More than 125 years old, the bridge is the only operational wooden viaduct in Wales. A pedestrian walkway follows alongside the rails. At Fairbourne, on the far side of the viaduct from Barmouth, a miniature steam railway allows visitors to take locomotives on a circular route and enjoy views of the sea and estuary. The line was originally constructed for the transportation of stone for the abutments of Barmouth Railway Bridge. Visitors can return to Barmouth by ferry across the bay.

MAWDDACH ESTUARY

The magnificent beauty of the Mawddach Estuary has been the inspiration for many writers and artists. Turner painted scenes here and Wordsworth described the estuary as "sublime", and comparable to the finest in Scotland. In 1869, Darwin wrote much of *The Descent of Man* in a house beside the estuary with views of Cadair Idris. The estuary runs 13km (8 miles) inland to Dolgellau and is the scene of spectacular sunsets. The Penmaenpool Toll Bridge is the next crossing after Barmouth Bridge at the river mouth. Found five miles (8km) upstream the wooden bridge, seen right, carries light traffic across the meandering Afon Mawddach.

HARLECH

Built by Edward I between 1283 and 1286, the commanding castle at Harlech almost grows from the rock on which it stands. Once, the waters of Tremadog Bay lapped the foot of the castle; today extensive sand dunes fringe the wide golden sands of Harlech Beach. The attractive town sits on a ridge behind the castle, a World Heritage Site, with breathtaking views from its narrow streets across the bay to the Lleyn peninsula and north towards Snowdonia.

DOLGELLAU

Thought to mean "meadow of the hazels", the small market town of Dolgellau is pleasantly situated beside the river Wnion. Beyond it lies the bulk of Cadair Idris. The town is full of narrow streets, and a seven-arched bridge over the river dates from the early 17th century. Before the town became a Victorian holiday resort to attract climbers to Cadair Idris, there was a small rural Quaker community in the area that emigrated to Pennsylvania due to persecution in 1686. A university in Pennsylvania is named Bryn Mawr after the home of Rowland Ellis, the local farmer who led the emigration, and a museum in Dolgellau is dedicated to the story.

CYMER ABBEY

Just north of Dolgellau lie the ruins of a 12th-century Cistercian abbey, near the village of Llanelltyd. It was a simple design and one of the smallest abbeys built in Wales. Though never completed, the abbey was heavily damaged during the Welsh wars of the 13th century. During Henry VIII's dissolution of the monasteries, a silver gilt chalice and paten were hidden in the nearby mountains and found in the 19th century.

MID WALES

The quiet valleys of mid Wales link Snowdonia in the north with the Brecon Beacons National Park in the south. Market towns such as Llanidloes, Builth Wells and Brecon cluster scenically around the rivers Severn, Wye and Usk. Elegant Georgian architecture is a feature of many mid Wales towns, while others such as Llandrindod Wells developed later in the Victorian era as spa resorts. In the 17th and 18th centuries the region was a heartland for the Welsh textile and flannel industry, with Newtown in particular referred to as the "Leeds of Wales". Most settlements lie to the east of the Cambrian mountains and have been involved in border disputes over the centuries. Many of the Mid Wales medieval castles were ruined in the Civil War; others have been converted into impressive fortified manor houses that can be visited today.

CHIRK

The National Trust property, Chirk Castle, lies two miles west of Chirk. The magnificent estate is entered through wrought iron gates and includes beautiful castle gardens. Construction of the rectangular castle began in the late 13th century on land granted to Roger de Mortimer by Edward I. Chirk Castle has been rebuilt on several occasions but still features its dramatic drum towers at each corner. The castle is still lived in today and the rather austere exterior belies the elegant state rooms with their eleborate plasterwork and fine furniture.

WREXHAM

Wrexham grew rapidly in the industrial 19th century. Though the town was the site of coalmining and ironworks, the brewing industry played a major role in shaping Wrexham's growth. Britain's first lager brewery was built in the town in 1882 and several other large breweries were based nearby. Brick and tile manufacturing added to Wrexham's commercial prosperity. The steeple of St Giles' Church, completed in 1506, overlooks the town in this photograph. The church is the burial place of Elihu Yale, the benefactor of Yale University.

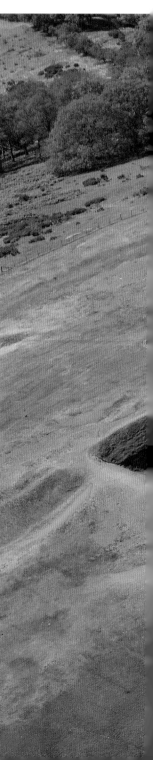

LLANGOLLEN

Llangollen is a dramatic entry point to Wales; the picturesque scenery of the river Dee and the rich history of the town have drawn visitors to the town for centuries. An elegant bridge built by Bishop Trevor dates from 1345 and was widened in the 1960s to accommodate modern traffic. Since 1947, Llangollen has hosted the annual International Eisteddfod every July, bringing the nations together to compete in folk dancing and singing. In 1955, a young Luciano Pavarotti sang as a member of an Italian male voice choir.

CASTELL DINAS BRAN

Also known as Crow Castle, the remains of this medieval castle are found high above Llangollen and can be seen for miles around. Views of the valley from the hilltop are breathtaking. The 13th-century castle built by the princes of Powys Fadog stands on the site of an earlier Iron Age hill fort. The kings of Powys are thought to have used the fort as a home until the 8th century. During the wars between Llwelyn ap Gruffydd, Prince of Wales, and Edward I of England, the castle was burnt by the Welsh before it was captured.

POWIS CASTLE

Situated close to Welshpool, Powis Castle is famous for its gardens and antiques. Originally built in the 13th century, the building has been added to over the years and reflects the tastes and styles of its various owners. It now resembles a large mansion house surrounded by gardens that include terraces, an orangery and informal woodlands that overlook the river Severn. The castle contains one of the finest collections of paintings and furniture in Wales. Clive of India's son, Edward, was a previous owner of the castle and the Clive Museum, located on the property, features treasures from his travels.

WELSHPOOL *right*

On the banks of the river Severn, close to the English border, lies Welshpool. Originally known as the Pool, a suffix was added in 1835 to remove any ambiguity over which side of the border the town was on. Leisurely trips can be enjoyed along the Montgomery canal, or on a 50-minute journey on the steam railway to Llanfair Caereinion. Welshpool has numerous half-timbered buildings and architectural features and the only surviving cockpit remaining on its original site in Wales. Built in the 18th century, the cockpit remained in use until the sport was banned in Britain in 1849.

VALLE CRUCIS ABBEY *left*

This Cistercian abbey is surrounded by steep-sided hills and woodland just north of Llangollen. Monks sought isolation at the abbey founded in 1201 by Madog ap Gruffyd, the Prince of Powys. Visitors can explore the site and get a feel of how the monks lived. The abbey is in good condition despite a fire, the collapse of the tower and the Dissolution of the Monasteries in the 16th century. Some mutilated tombs are thought to include that of Iolo Goch, a bard of Owain Glyndŵr. Valle Crucis means Abbey of the Cross and refers to a pillar erected in the 9th century that stands a mile from the site.

MONTGOMERY *left*

Some of the best-preserved sections of Offa's Dyke lie close to Montgomery, the town that gave the county of Montgomeryshire its name. This attractive market town has a number of fine Georgian buildings and is the site of a ruined borderland castle on a hill overlooking the town. The castle was first built in the early 13th century but was stormed by rebels over the years. It was demolished in 1649 after it was surrendered to Parliamentarians during the Civil War.

NEWTOWN

Founded in the 10th century, Newtown is the home of the newsagent WH Smith and features a museum of the company's history and growth. Originally the town was a centre for textiles and weaving and became the home of the Welsh flannel industry. The Textile Museum tells the story of the industry that led to Newtown being referred to as "the Leeds of Wales". The social reformer Robert Owen (1771-1858) grew up here and decided to spend his life improving working conditions in industry.

ELAN VALLEY
Dramatic dams and reservoirs can be found throughout the Elan Valley. Built at the end of the 19th century to supply water to the West Midlands, the reservoirs are set among the spectacular scenery of the Cambrian mountains. These hills are home to one of Britain's most rare and beautiful birds – the Red Kite.

RHAYADER
Rhayader, which is situated on the upper river Wye, is often called the Gateway to the Lakeland of Wales as it stands close to the impressive flooded Elan Valley. The waterfall that lies on the river just below the town bridge gave the town its name – Rhaeadr Gwy (waterfall on the Wye). The town dates back to the 5th century and contains a 12th-century castle.

LLANIDLOES

The first Welsh market town on the river Severn, Llanidloes is a great base for hiking in the Cambrian mountains. The town was founded by St Idloes in the 7th century and began to expand after the construction of a motte and bailey castle by the Normans. The main streets were laid out in the shape of a cross, with the Old Market Hall placed at the centre in the 1600s. This beautiful, half-timbered building still stands. The town became known as a centre of the flannel industry in the 17th and 18th centuries and during the depression of the 1830s a riot lasted for five days until order was restored by troops. The town was occupied for an entire year. In the 20th century a lead-smelting industry developed and the population doubled.

BUILTH WELLS

The spa town of Builth Wells is situated beside the river Wye in South Powys. A beautiful six-arched bridge crosses the river beside the town. In this photograph, the castle mound can be seen, a short distance from the town centre. Originally a Norman motte and bailey castle, it was later replaced by a 13th-century castle and all that remains now are the earthworks. During the late 19th century, visitors began to visit the town to "take the waters".

ROYAL WELSH SHOWGROUND *right*

In nearby Llanelwedd, across the river Wye, lies the Royal Welsh Showground. Opened in 1963, the showground was built to accommodate the Royal Welsh Show, which takes place each July and brings the farming communities of Wales together. The show, which is now the largest agricultural show in Europe, takes place over four days and attracts 200,000 visitors annually. Events include sheepdog trials, riding competitions, falconry and cattle judging.

LLANDRINDOD WELLS

The most famous of the mid Wales spas is Llandrindod Wells, a town of largely
Victorian and Edwardian architecture. Although there is evidence of Roman
occupation, it was not until the Victorian era that the healing benefits of its spa
waters meant that the town developed as a major visitor attraction. At its peak some
80,000 visitors arrived each year to take the waters and cure ailments such as gout,
rheumatism and dyspepsia. It is still possible to use the spas at the Pump House in
Rock Park. The town, affectionately known as Llandod, grew up around Rock Park
and Pump House Hotel alongside the spa waters in 1747. Today there are no pubs in
the town centre, but there are bars in the town's hotels and inns.

HAY-ON-WYE

The ancient town of Hay-on-Wye is famous for its
secondhand bookshops. They first opened in 1961 and
since then many other book, print and craft shops have
sprung up around the town. Hay is also the site of an
annual festival of art and literature, which attracts a
wide range of authors each May. The town, situated
beside the river Wye and the Black Mountains, lies at
the northernmost corner of the Brecon Beacons
National Park and includes the remains of a Norman
castle destroyed by Owain Glyndŵr.

TRETOWER CASTLE

The medieval buildings of Tretower Castle and Tretower
Court in the Usk Valley can be seen in this photograph.
Only the castle's 13th-century keep survives, built on a
Norman motte. The court is a fortified manor house
with magnificent gardens kept in the 15th-century style.

BRECON

Brecon lies on the banks of the River Usk and grew up around its famous cathedral. Founded in the 11th century, the building was originally the Priory Church of St John the Evangelist and was given cathedral status in 1923. Brecon is also the site of medieval castle ruins, an annual jazz festival and the Monmouthshire and Brecon Canal.

LLANGORSE

Llangorse Lake (Llyn Syfaddan) is the largest natural lake in Wales, with a shoreline over four miles (6km) long. In medieval times the waters were thought to have healing properties and many legends are linked to the lake.

BRECON BEACONS

The Brecon Beacons National Park is named after this distinctively-shaped sandstone mountain ridge, just south of Brecon. The last of the three Welsh national parks, it was formed in 1957. Pen y Fan, at 2907ft (886m), is the highest peak in the Brecon Beacons range and is known as the most dangerous mountain in Wales for its rapidly changing weather conditions. The range extends westward to Corn Du at 2864ft (873m) and Cribyn beyond at 2608ft (795m). Fan y Bîg lies to the east and reaches 2359ft (719 m). The national park is over 500sq miles (1344sq km) in area and includes two other mountain ranges.

CRICKHOWELL

Crickhowell is a popular base for hikers in the Black Mountains and is situated in a beautiful valley in the Brecon Beacons National Park beside the river Usk. The small town is named after an Iron Age fort known as Crug Hywell (Howell's Fort) that once stood on a flat-topped hill overlooking the town. Evidence of the ditch and ramparts can still be seen. A beautiful 17th-century bridge crosses the river beside the town and features, uniquely, 13 arches on one side and 12 on the other. There is also a castle, built in the 11th century, of which only the motte and two towers remain.

SOUTH WALES

South Wales is home to the largest cities in Wales, including the capital city, Cardiff. Newport, Swansea and Cardiff all developed rapidly during the 19th century as busy ports exporting coal and iron ore from the South Wales valleys. Canals, then rail networks, were used to transport coal to the dockyards. Coastal resorts such as Porthcawl and Mumbles offered respite from work in the factories and mines, while the scenic Gower peninsula remained largely untouched. Some magnificent castles are found in the region including Norman strongholds at Coity and Ogmore and the impressive 13th-century fortification at Caerphilly.

RAGLAN

Construction of the magnificent Raglan Castle which lies south-west of Monmouth began in 1435 on the site of a former Norman motte and bailey castle. The stronghold is regarded as the last "true" castle to be built in Britain. Sir William ap Thomas, who fought with King Henry V at the Battle of Agincourt, designed the building. He built an unusual hexagonal keep surrounded by its own moat called "The Great Tower". Initially, the building was constructed with local yellowish sandstone, but later ap Thomas' son, William Herbert, added a significant amount of Tudor styling in Old Red sandstone. William Herbert also built formal state apartments and an impressive gatehouse. The castle survived one of the longest sieges of the Civil War but fell into ruin soon after.

ABERGAVENNY

Popular in the summer months, Abergavenny is a pleasant base for pony-trekking, canal trips and walks in the Brecon Beacons. Situated in the picturesque Usk valley, this small market town is the site of a former Roman fort. A Norman castle built in the town shortly after the Norman Conquest saw a great deal of action due to the town's location close to the English border. The Norman lord William de Braose (known as the Ogre of Abergavenny) held the lordship here during a treacherous period of murder and cruelty in the 12th century. A museum in the castle's restored keep and hunting lodge tells the story of both the castle and the local area from prehistoric times.

CHEPSTOW
Situated on the river Wye, this border town retains a number of medieval features including the town walls, town gate and narrow streets. A thriving commercial centre, Chepstow's name comes from the Old English *ceap stow* meaning "market town". The well-preserved Chepstow Castle, built by the Normans, overlooks the river and was probably the first stone-built medieval castle in Britain. Offa's Dyke starts in Chepstow and marks a physical border that reaches to the very north of Wales.

LLANDOGO *right*
Between Monmouth and Chepstow, close to the English border, lies Llandogo. This pretty village is situated on steep ground by the banks of the river Wye. Cleddon Falls, in the grounds of Cleddon Hall, overlook the village and are surrounded by attractive scenery.

TINTERN ABBEY *right*

The magnificent ruins of Tintern Abbey have inspired artists and writers for centuries, including Turner and Wordsworth. Great soaring archways hint at the original splendour of this wealthy abbey. Nestled among the wooded slopes of the Wye valley in a designated area of outstanding natural beauty, the abbey was founded by Cistercian monks in the 12th century and largely rebuilt by Roger Bigod, the Lord of Chepstow Castle in the 13th century. The great church was added between 1269 and 1301. Now roofless and lacking internal walls (these were removed in Victorian times), the abbey is a romantic and impressive sight. King Henry VIII's Dissolution of the Monasteries in the 16th century brought an end to the monastic way of life at Tintern Abbey and the building was surrendered in 1536.

MONMOUTH

A five-arched bridge built in 1617 spans the river Wye beside the charming market town of Monmouth. The town is situated at the confluence of three rivers with the river Monnow to the left of the town centre. It is crossed by the famous Monnow Bridge, which features the last remaining medieval gatehouse in Britain which is on the bridge itself. A Norman castle built in the town was the birthplace of Henry V in 1387, and a Great Castle House constructed from the ruins in the 17th century now houses a castle and regimental museum. The Nelson Museum also contains interesting artefacts relating to the life of the famous maritime commander.

NEWPORT

Although Newport has an ancient history, dating back to the Romans, the town is best known for its industrial heritage. The discovery of coal and iron ore in the Monmouthshire valleys led to Newport's sudden development from a small village to a world-famous port. By the 1830s the population had grown tenfold and Newport was the largest town in Wales. The industrial wealth from the valleys was brought to an inland dock by canals and steam power. While

Newport has seen the decline of traditional industries in the 20th century, it now serves new industries. The massive transporter bridge to the right was built in 1906 and is believed to be one of only five other such bridges in the world. It was designed to allow shipping to continue along the river Usk uninterrupted by the flow of traffic across the bridge. The history of the docks is explored at the Pillgwenlly Heritage Centre.

NEWPORT RUGBY

Rodney Parade, which stands on the east bank of the river Usk, is the home ground of Newport Rugby Football Club and also Newport Gwent Dragons – one of the four professional regional rugby sides in Wales.

The Welfare Ground (right) is home to Newbridge Rugby Football Club. The club was formed in 1888 and moved to The Welfare in 1925. Former members include Welsh international players Paul Turner and Andrew Gibbs. The ground is shared with Newbridge Cricket Club.

CARDIFF

Wales' capital city, situated beside the Bristol Channel, is a vibrant and exciting metropolis with a rich history. A small town until the early 19th century, Cardiff grew rapidly during the industrial revolution and is today the largest city in Wales. The photograph (right) shows an impressive view of Cardiff's Millennium Stadium, built next to Cardiff's Arms Park rugby ground in 1999. It is the national stadium of Wales and features an 8,000 ton retractable roof, the first to be built in the UK. Visitors to the stadium can discover how the roof opens and closes, walk through the tunnel from the players' dressing room onto the pitch and find out how it was laid. Many important games have been held here including the Rugby World Cup Final in 1999, and a number of FA Cup Finals. The stadium cost £126m to construct and has also hosted concerts and the British Speedway Grand Prix.

CARDIFF DOCKS

During the 19th century, Cardiff's port – known as Tiger Bay – was one of the world's busiest, exporting coal around the world. The Bute family controlled the docks and spent some of their vast fortune improving the town including a major investment in rebuilding Cardiff Castle. Inside the grounds of the castle some of the original medieval remains can be seen, but much of the construction is representative of Victorian opulence. Tiger Bay housed one of the UK's earliest immigrant communities, with Shirley Bassey as its most famous resident. The historic dockland has recently been regenerated and renamed Cardiff Bay. After years of decline, the once notorious neighbourhood is now an attractive waterfront location with shops, harbourside apartments, restaurants and offices. A new building for the National Assembly for Wales was designed by Richard Rogers and opened in 2006 by the Queen.

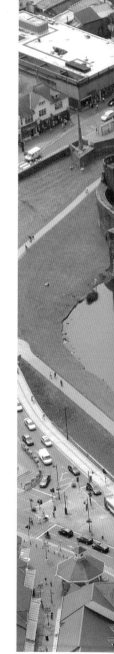

CARDIFF CIVIC CENTRE

The civic area of Cardiff, Cathays Park contains a number of early 20th-century buildings set amidst 60 acres of beautifully laid out parkland. Just north-east of the castle, these include civic buildings, departments of the University of Wales, City Hall (with its domed roof topped with a dragon), the National Museum and Gallery of Wales and the law courts. Some of the finest civic buildings were constructed in elegant Edwardian-style with Portland stone imported from Dorset. The National Museum holds an especially impressive collection of art, archaeology and natural history, and has a large collection of 18th-century porcelain. Cardiff University, with its famous medical school and faculty of law, is a world-renowned centre of education. The area around Cathays Park is home to many of the 25,000 students who attend the university.

LLANDAFF CATHEDRAL *left*

Beside the River Taff in the suburb of Llandaff lies the cathedral, built on a site of pilgrimage since the sixth century. The cathedral has been ruined and restored a number of times over the centuries. Following the Norman Conquest, construction began in 1120 on a cathedral to replace the existing monastic settlement, and 170 years after work began, the building was completed. The cathedral was attacked by Owain Glyndŵr during the 1400 revolt, but restored by Jasper Tudor shortly afterwards. It was stormed by Parliamentarian forces during the Civil War, and restored again during the 19th century. In the Second World War, the cathedral suffered severe bomb damage; restoration was completed in 1958.

CAERPHILLY

Spread over 30 acres, Caerphilly Castle is the largest castle in Wales and the second largest in Britain (after Windsor Castle). Built in the late 13th century by the Norman Lord Gilbert de Clare, it is an example of a concentric castle with impressive defence systems. As well as walls within walls, the fortress is surrounded by an impressive moat and a number of lake and island arrangements to deter and slow attackers. The castle also features a leaning tower that was a victim of attacks by Parliamentary forces in 1648; interestingly, it out-performs the famous tower in Pisa. Unlike other Welsh castles, Caerphilly was largely untouched during the Civil War. Much of the castle was restored in the 19th century by the Marquess of Bute.

PONTYPRIDD *left*

The valleys of south-west Wales that lie inland from Cardiff were famous the world over for mining and the export of coal and iron. Clustered around the rivers Rhondda, Cynon and Taff, towns such as Pontypridd and Merthyr Tydfil grew rapidly during the 19th century in a landscape of coal heaps and deep-mine pit heads. Densely packed Victorian terraces were built to house the thousands of miners that lived in the region.

EBBW VALE *below*

The Ebbw Vale Iron Works (later known as the Ebbw Vale Steelworks) opened in the late 18th century and transformed Ebbw Vale and the surrounding area. The population grew almost tenfold in the first 15 years, and business reached its peak in the 1930s. The steelworks were the largest in Europe and survived the bombing of the Second World War.

TOWER COLLIERY *above*
The miners who worked the last deep mine in South Wales were made redundant when Tower Colliery closed in 1994. But the following year, the employees bought out and re-opened the colliery. It is now the only worker-owned coalmine in Europe.

MERTHYR TYDFIL *right*
Once the iron capital of the world, this town at the Heads of the Valleys (population 55,000) is moving on from its industrial past; new businesses have relocated to the area, attracted by many regeneration initiatives.

RHONDDA HERITAGE PARK

Based in the former Lewis Merthyr Colliery, the Rhondda Heritage Park provides visitors with an experience of mining life. Though the Rhondda valley is just 16 miles long, it contained 53 working collieries at its peak. The heritage park is situated in Trehafod, in the lower reaches of the Rhondda Valley. The mine prospered with easy access to the Glamorgan Canal, and later to the Taff Vale Railway en route to Cardiff. The Glamorgan Canal, constructed in the late 18th century, was 25 miles long; a major engineering feat, the canal required 50 locks but little remains today. After the First World War, industry began to decline in the area. Coal winding ceased at Lewis Merthyr in 1958 shortly after a terrible explosion at the colliery that killed nine men and injured five others. Many deep mines closed in the 1980s and production ceased at Lewis Merthyr Colliery in 1983. By 1990 the colliery had been converted into a historic landmark. Some open-cast mines remain in the Welsh valleys today, particularly in the north.

COITY CASTLE

The embankments and curtain walls of the castle at
Coity dwarf the small, quiet village. Though the castle
is one of three Norman strongholds in the area, along
with Newcastle and Ogmore, much of the standing
stonework was built in the 14th century by Sir Payn de
Turberville. Sir Lawrence Berkerolles ordered substantial
alterations to the keep and castle. New buildings were
added within the inner bailey as well as new walls,
towers, a portcullis and a drawbridge. Further
embellishments were added during Tudor times such as
tall chimneys rising from the kitchen. The once-mighty
castle managed to withstand a siege by the Welsh rebel,
Owain Glyndŵr, in the early 15th century when others
crumbled. However, the castle fell into disrepair when
it was abandoned in the 17th century and is now
maintained by CADW (the Welsh Assembly's historic
environment division). Entry to the castle is free.

OGMORE

The remains of Ogmore Castle can be seen on the south side of the
river Ewenny beside a ford across the river in a green and peaceful
location. The castle was first built by the Norman, William de
Londres, in the early 12th century and added to by his family in the
13th century. There are extensive ruins at the site but the dry moat
and three-storey keep still stand. The buildings are said to be haunted
by a ghost known as The White Lady (Y Ladi Wen). She guards
treasure thought to be buried at the site.

NEATH

The first copper smelter in Wales was built here in the 16th century by Cornishmen, and marks the beginning of the town's strong industrial heritage. Located at a crossing point of the river Neath, the town was founded by St Illtyd, a Celtic saint, after the Roman occupation of Britain ended in the fifth century. Neath expanded during the Industrial Revolution and was a major transportation centre for coal mined in the surrounding valleys. The town is now a commercial centre and tourist attraction.

NEATH ABBEY

The abbey at Neath was originally built by the Norman Baron Richard de Granville on land that had been seized from the Welsh in the early 12th century. In the 16th century, the building was converted into a mansion by Sir Richard Williams and passed on to Sir John Herbert. It remained occupied throughout the 17th century and later became a copper smelting and casting workshop. Remains of a Roman town can be visited close to the ruins of the abbey.

PORTHCAWL

The attractive harbour nestles close to the headland by Rest Bay in the popular seaside resort of Porthcawl. Now famous for its clean wide beaches at Sandy Bay, Trecco Bay and Rest Bay, Porthcawl was once a busy port exporting coal and iron. The Edwardian promenade dates from this time and there are many historic buildings around the harbour. The port's growth was soon overtaken by other rapidly-growing ports such as Barry and so the focus turned to tourism. The Grand Pavilion was built in the 1930s and was once one of the most popular pantomime venues in Wales. It hosts an Elvis festival each year, known as the Elvies, attracting Elvis impersonators from around the world. Visitors come to Porthcawl for both relaxation and non-stop entertainment. There are amusement arcades, white-knuckle rides and family activities, as well as surfing, sailing, fishing and golf. The town has become famous for brave swimmers who face the bracing waters of the Bristol Channel each year on Christmas Day.

PORT TALBOT

A deep water harbour was opened in 1970 by the Queen and serves Port Talbot's steel industry. It is the deepest harbour in the Severn Estuary and is mainly used to import raw materials such as iron ore. Port Talbot has many factories and processing plants and has been an industrial area for centuries, with a long history of coalmining. The town is named after the Talbot family who developed the original harbour in the 19th century.

SWANSEA

Shipbuilding and coalmining were important industries in Swansea from as early as the 14th century. The port soon became the largest in Wales and a copper industry sprang up with the arrival of smelters from Cornwall. At one point, 90 per cent of Britain's copper came from Swansea and it was nicknamed Copperopolis. With the decline of traditional industry, the old dock at Swansea was converted into a marina and the lively maritime quarter is now packed with cafes and bars. Swansea Castle can be seen in the photograph on the right, hemmed in by modern buildings in the city centre.

SWANSEA

At the mouth of the River Tawe (its Welsh name is Abertawe), Swansea is the wettest city in Britain but its location by the coast gives it a milder climate than the inland mountains and valleys. Little remains of the medieval city centre apart from some of the road layouts. The city experienced heavy bombing during the Second World War and the centre was flattened completely. This photograph shows Mount Pleasant, an area of steep narrow streets on the hill north of Swansea's city centre.

MUMBLES

Mumbles Lighthouse
stands on the headland at
Mumbles at the western
end of the wide Swansea
Bay. Built in 1794, it warns
ships of two massive
underwater sandbanks
close by. The Victorian
pier has been restored and
houses a café and
amusement arcade.
Mumbles is the gateway to
the Gower coast and the
seas here are popular with
the sailing community.
The village developed
around the fishing
community at
Oystermouth; the name
Mumbles comes from the
French word *mamelles*,
meaning breasts, a
reference to the two
islands beyond the
promontory.

OYSTERMOUTH

The hill on which
Oystermouth Castle stands
allows visitors fantastic views
eastwards across Swansea Bay
and west towards the glorious
beaches of the Gower
peninsula. The castle was
founded by the Normans in
the early 12th century and its
main sections were built in
the 13th and 14th centuries.
The stronghold is now in
ruins but is a popular tourist
destination with an open-air
theatre in the grounds during
the summer months.
Oystermouth was once a
small fishing village but
developed into a seaside
resort in the Victorian era.

PENRICE CASTLE *below*

The ivy-covered ruin of Penrice is the largest castle on the Gower peninsula; from its wooded slopes there are panoramic views over Oxwich Bay. Set in the heart of the Gower, in an area of outstanding natural beauty, the castle was built by a Norman named de Penres. It was constructed on the motte of a previous castle built in 1090 and most of the existing walls were built in the 13th century. In front of the castle stands a neo-Classical Georgian mansion built in the 1770s by Thomas Mansel Talbot, whose family owned the estate. Mansel Talbot employed William Eames, a pupil of Capability Brown, to landscape the gardens. He laid out a number of lakes, walks and kitchen gardens which can still be seen today. Later, in the 1790s, an orangery and a gatehouse were added.

CASWELL BAY

The first major resort west of Mumbles, Caswell Bay is a beautiful area with a wide sandy beach. In certain weather conditions the beach is popular with surfers. The resort's popularity grew in Victorian times when it was regularly visited by groups of children from workhouses. Today, lifeguards patrol the area during high season and a dog ban in the summer helps to keep the beach clean and safe for bathing.

OXWICH

Oxwich is the largest bay on Gower's south-facing coast. Overlooking the bay on its western headland lies Oxwich Castle, a Tudor manor house built by Sir Rice Mansel in the 1520s on the site of a former stronghold. His son added to the building, but it fell into disrepair soon afterwards and only some sections remain. At low tide, visitors can walk along the wide expanse of sand towards Tor Bay, Three Cliffs Bay and Pobbles Bay.

WHITEFORD POINT

Beyond the dune and pine plantation at Whiteford Burrows just north of Llanmadoc lies a glorious sandy beach, two miles long, at the southern edge of the Loughor Estuary. At the tip of Whiteford Point, stands an old lighthouse that can be reached on foot at low tide. The journey is long and can be treacherous due to changing tides and quicksands – unexploded shells add a further hazard for the unwary hiker. Now a listed ancient monument, the lighthouse was used for bomb practice during the First World War. From here, the visitor can enjoy views across the estuary towards Llanelli.

WORMS HEAD *right*

The nature reserve on Worms Head can be reached across the causeway at low tide. Rising tides can make this crossing dangerous and a large bell is available to those who get into difficulties. The island lies at the westernmost tip of the Gower peninsula, close to the village of Rhossili. Owned by the National Trust, Worms Head contains a bird reserve and there are a number of shipwrecks to see at low tide, including the *Helvetia* which dates from 1887. There are panoramic views from Rhossili Downs over the three-mile long beach – the longest on the Gower Peninsula.

LLANELLI

The town of Llanelli is famous for its industry and its rugby. Steel, tin-plating, chemical and engineering works are just some of the heavy industries based here. Llanelli is home to the Scarlets, one of the most renowned of the Welsh rugby teams. The team's anthem, *Sospan Fach* (meaning "little saucepan"), is a Welsh folksong and a reminder of the area's industrial heritage.

STRADEY CASTLE

Stradey Castle is the Llanelli home of the Mansel-Lewis family. Though close to the mud and sands of the Loughor Estuary and the centre of Llanelli, the mansion backs onto woodland beside the Afon Dulais. Today's mansion was built to replace an earlier building from the 17th century, moving the estate to higher ground. Its turrets and towers and grand appearance have attracted film crews to the area. The interior of the building has recently been used as the film set for a remake of *Heidi*, featuring the actor Diana Rigg.

BURRY HOLMS

The tidal island of Burry Holms which lies at the western end of the Gower peninsula was an inland hill 12 miles from the sea in prehistoric times. Today it is rich in archaeological finds including tools made of flint, wood and bone along with charcoal from local woodland.

LLANRHIDIAN SANDS

To the east of Whiteford Sands, on the east side of the Loughor Estuary, lie the Llanrhidian Sands and saltmarshes. The marshes are a good site for spotting oystercatchers and little egret. The Loughor Estuary is famous for its seafood and most of the cockle-picking industry is located in the villages of Crofty and Llanmorlais.

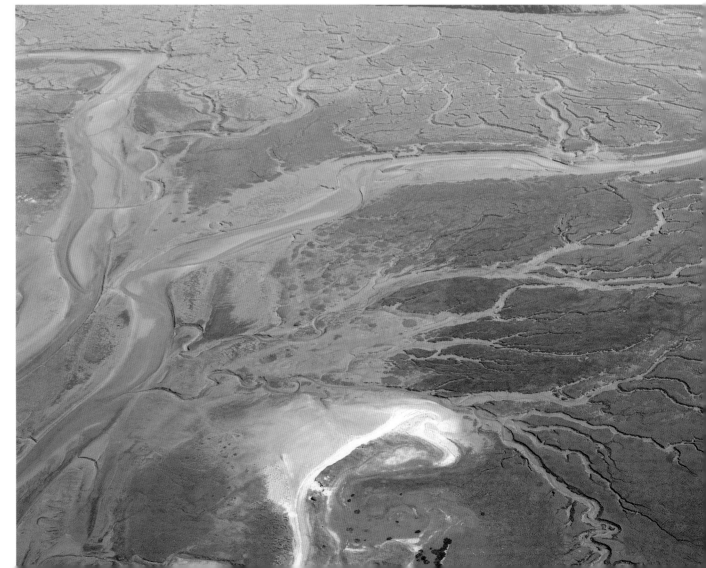

LAUGHARNE

The village of Laugharne lies on the banks of the Tâf estuary. The picturesque Laugharne Castle (above) was originally an earth and timber construction; by the 13th century it had been rebuilt in stone and its fortifications were further improved in the 16th century by Sir John Perrot. The castle fell into ruin after a siege during the Civil War. The Victorian garden has been restored and was the inspiration for a dramatic watercolour by Turner. Just north of the castle lies the distinctive white-painted town hall, which can be clearly seen in the photograph.

Laugharne is famous as the place where the poet Dylan Thomas (1914-1953) settled for the last four years of his life. Thomas lived at the Boathouse with his wife Caitlin and his three children. Close to the edge of the estuary the Boathouse (right) can be seen on the bottom left of the photograph. The home was gifted to the poet by Margaret Taylor who wanted Thomas to remain in Wales. Whilst at Laugharne, the poet would write in a shed in the Boathouse garden; here he wrote many of his best works including *Under Milk Wood* in which the famous village of Llareggub drew much of its inspiration from Laugharne. The Boathouse is now a heritage centre; Dylan and Caitlin are buried in the churchyard of St Martin's church in the village.

LLANDOVERY *right*

This ancient drovers' town in Carmarthenshire is based in the Brecon Beacons National Park. Now a small market town, its attractions include the delightful ruins of a Norman castle, a heritage park and Llandovery College. The town is associated with two famous Welshmen – the hymn writer, William Williams, and the outlaw, Twm Siôn Cati.

CARMARTHEN *right*

Carmarthen is a centre for agriculture in the region and one of the oldest Roman settlements in Wales. A Roman amphitheatre remains and the Roman walls, believed to date from AD75-77, were visible until the 12th century. The famous magician Merlin is said to be a native of Carmarthen and the town has been known as Caer-Merlin. The County Hall can be seen in this photograph, built on the site of Carmarthen Prison and Castle. The castle was originally constructed by the Normans, but few traces remain today.

South-west & West Wales

Established in 1952, the Pembrokeshire Coast National Park is Britain's only truly coastal national park and is a major attraction in south-west Wales. Its rugged cliffs and sandy beaches provide a home for a diverse range of wildlife. Islands along the coast include the remote monastic community of Caldey Island and bird sanctuaries at Skomer and Skokholm. The harbours at Milford Haven, Fishguard and Pembroke Dock gave the region strategic importance. The Victorian statesman, Lord Palmerston, protected these with a number of mid-19th century island forts. Every year visitors flock to the region's scenic coastline with resorts such as Tenby, St Davids and Pembroke, and further west to the stately town of Aberystwyth.

Caldey Island
Situated in Carmarthen Bay, a short distance off the coast of Tenby, Caldey Island has been the centre of a monastic community for over 1,500 years. It is possible to make a day trip across Caldey Sound to the island in summer to visit the abbey, the old priory with its leaning tower and St Davids, the island's parish church. The little post office allows visitors to have postcards franked with the unique Caldey imprint.

TENBY

Quaint pastel-coloured Georgian houses surround the harbour at Tenby. At the edge of the harbour lies Castle Hill, and behind it is St Catherine's Island on which the 19th-century St Catherine's Fort stands. Little remains of the castle after which the headland is named, but the views of Carmarthen Bay from the promontory are superb. Much of the town's medieval development is still apparent, including winding lanes and 13th-century town walls. St Catherine's Fort was built in the 1860s to protect the Pembrokeshire coast from the threat of a French invasion. It saw no action and was sold off shortly afterwards.

ST MARGARET'S ISLAND

At the western end of Caldey Island lies St Margaret's Island. A seal and bird sanctuary, the island has no public access. It is home to the largest population of cormorants in Wales (three per cent of the British population). St Margaret's is named after a chapel that once stood on the headland, which was converted into housing for quarry-workers in Victorian times. In this photograph, the two islands are viewed from Caldey Sound, with St Margaret's in the foreground and Caldey to the rear. Priory Beach, the place where ferries from Tenby dock on Caldey is seen on the left of the main island. Sandtop Bay on the western shore can be clearly seen on the right. On the far side of Caldey Island is the lighthouse which was built in 1829. Along with Lundy North lighthouse it helps shipping to navigate the Bristol Channel in safety. In 1927 the lighthouse was converted to an automatic gas system and looked after by a part-time attendant; in 1997 it was fulled automated and converted to mains electricity. Caldey is completely traffic-free and must be explored on foot. There are wonderful views of the Pembrokeshire coast from high points above the landing point on Priory Beach.

CALDEY ATTRACTIONS

The monastery overlooks the village green on Caldey. Its abbey has distinctive white walls and red-tiled roofs and is now a grade II listed building. Designed in traditional Italianate-style by Penarth architect John Coates-Carter, under the direction of the Anglican Benedictines, the abbey was constructed in 1910. The Anglican Benedictines were forced to move on shortly afterwards owing to financial difficulties. Today Cistercian monks have made their home on the island, beside the cottages owned by islanders. About 20 monks live in the monastery and attend seven services throughout the day. They are also involved in farming and make and sell dairy products. Perfumes produced by the monks reflect the flowers, gorse and herbs of Caldey island. The Perfumery Shop is world famous and a popular stop for visitors. Tours are available, but due to the strict Rule of St Benedict by which the monks lead their lives, women are not allowed to enter the monastery.

PEMBROKE *above*

Pembroke Castle is one of the great strongholds of Britain, used by the Normans as a base for their Irish campaign. During the late 12th century, William Marshall, a Welsh Marcher lord, replaced the earth and timber fortress with stone fortifications, creating a mighty gatehouse tower. The surrounding walls were 19ft (almost 6m) thick and 75ft (22m) high. This strength as well as the castle's ideal location – on a high ridge between two tidal inlets of the river Cleddau – meant that the castle was a formidable defence against attacks by the Welsh. Domestic buildings were added and improved in the 13th century and in the 14th century the castle was handed to the crown. Henry Tudor – later to become Henry VII – was born here in 1547. On-site exhibitions tell the history of the castle and King Henry's story. The medieval town grew up around the castle and docks. Some sections of the 13th-century town walls still stand.

PEMBROKE DOCK *right*

Pembroke Dock was created in 1814, a ferry port and Royal Naval Dockyard three miles north of Pembroke. The town grew rapidly as shipbuilding took off. Workers were skilled in the construction of wooden battleships and crowds flocked to the launches of newly-built ships. The arrival of the age of iron meant the end for Pembroke Dock, which was located miles from any suitable ironworks. The dockyard finally closed in 1926 but restored Georgian and Victorian buildings, such as the dockyard chapel and the Gun Tower museum, are evidence of Pembroke's former naval glories.

The Defensible Barracks (right) stand on a hill overlooking the dockyard. Built between 1841 and 1846 by Lord Palmerston, to protect the dockyard from attack by the French, the structure is based on an unusual 16th-century Italian design. Water was stored in a huge underground reservoir so that troops could hold out successfully under a long seige.

CAREW CASTLE

East of Pembroke, on the flat land around the tidal reaches of the Carew river, stands the magnificent ruins of this stronghold which combined the mighty defences of a medieval fortress with the grandeur of a Tudor mansion. The castle commands a strong defensive position at a crossing point on the river which would have been navigable in the past.

Carew Castle was built between 1280 and 1310 and developed into a manor house with both Norman and Elizabethan influences. Archaeological remains found in the vicinity of the castle, beside the stunning 23-acre mill pond, suggest that the region was inhabited some 2,000 years ago. An Iron Age fort has been unearthed as well as Roman pottery. Close to the castle is the only restored tidal mill in Wales, a 19th-century building that replaced previous mills on the site dating from the 16th century. Also within the castle grounds is an impressive 11th-century Celtic cross and a medieval bridge.

MILFORD DOCKS

The area surrounding the natural harbour of Milford Haven developed into a major oil port during the 1960s and is still used by the leading oil companies. At 10 miles (16km) long and at some points up to two miles wide, the harbour offers superb shelter for large ships. Nelson described Milford Haven as "the finest port in Christendom" and shipping has been a major force in this area for centuries. Norsemen used the harbour, and King John set sail from here to conquer Ireland. The main docks were completed in the late 19th century and the port became a leading centre for fishing. Convoys rested here during the First and Second World Wars.

MILFORD HAVEN

The town was developed by Charles Francis Greville, under orders from his uncle Sir William Hamilton, who owned two manors nearby and saw the potential of Milford Haven as a port. Greville developed the town on the American grid-iron system that can still be seen today. The town is the largest in the county of Pembrokeshire with a population of just under 14,000. The Pembrokeshire Coast National Park now passes right through the town. In the days of Milford Haven's great fishing industry it was possible to walk the length of the docks on the decks of trawlers. Today a large marina occupies part of the dock basin and is a base for pleasurecraft. Local fishing boats still use the facilities, together with trawlers from Spain and Belgium.

SOUTH HOOK FORT *left*

After the Napoleonic Wars of the early 19th century
relations deteriorated between France and Britain.
Lord Palmerston built, constructed and modernised
over 70 forts and fortresses around the coast to protect
major ports in the event of an invasion. In case Ireland
fell to France, a number of forts were also built on the
west coast in the 1860s. These forts have been
nicknamed "Palmerston's follies" as they were never
used. A number surround the naval port of Milford
Haven including South Hook Fort.

STACK ROCK FORT *below*

Built between 1859 and 1861, Stack Rock Fort was
disarmed in 1929 and sold in 2005 after being placed
on the market for £150,000. Just off the coast from
South Hook Point, the island is situated in the
Pembrokeshire Marine Area of Conservation. Though
this is one of the most diverse marine communities in
the UK, it was badly affected by the *Sea Empress*
disaster of 1996 when 72,000 tons of crude oil were
released into the water.

THORN ISLAND FORT *left*

Built on the south side of the estuary, Thorn Island
Fort was converted into a hotel but its present use is
unknown. Situated beside West Angle Bay in the
Pembrokeshire National Park, the fort was the first in
the area to be built. The coastline is part of an area of
complex geological structures, and the foreshore is
home to a wide variety of flora and fauna.
Archaeological digs have uncovered a number of
burial sites in the vicinity.

SKOMER

This scene takes in a striking view of the Marloes Peninsula, Midland Isle and The Neck. Between Midland Isle and the peninsula is a tidal strait known as Jack Sound, about 1,970ft (600m) wide. It is famous for its strong and changeable currents and isolates Skomer Island from the mainland. From Wooltack Point on the mainland, only a fragment of Skomer can be seen. A number of sites around the islands are visited by scuba divers.

SKOKHOLM *left*

Just one square kilometre in size, Skokholm lies just south of Skomer. It is an uninhabited island famous for its red sandstone cliffs and abundant seabirds. The island is a nature reserve like its neighbour Skomer and was made famous by RM Lockley, an ornithologist who lived on the island while researching and writing about puffins and shearwaters. The white building is the Head, the island's lighthouse, constructed in 1861.

ST DAVIDS

Nestling within the Pembrokeshire Coast National Park, the small city of St Davids is a peaceful place famous for its 12th-century cathedral. The city was a site of pilgrimage for centuries, with thousands travelling to the shrine of St David, the patron saint of Wales. Legend has it that St David, born in the 6th century during the great age of saints, founded a monastery here. The cathedral was later built on the site and there is a shrine to the saint in the cathedral. A church named after the saint's mother, St Non, also lies close by. The ruins of the medieval Bishop's Palace lie adjacent to the cathedral.

ST DAVIDS HEAD

Situated in one of Wales's sunniest spots, St Davids Head is surrounded by wildlife. Dolphins and porpoises can be seen in the water, gannets and the occasional peregrine falcon in the sky, and plenty of wildflowers and marine grasses on the beaches and headlands. On the main promontory amongst the bracken, scrub and heather is evidence of an Iron Age settlement. A cromlech known as Croetan Arthur stands close to the remains of round stone huts and a field system by the hill of Carn Llidi. There are spectacular views from here, taking in Ramsey Island and, beyond, the islands known as Bishops and Clerks. To reach the promontory visitors must park beside the wide expanse of Whitesands Bay, also known as Porth Mawr, and walk alongside two further beaches, Porthmeigan and Porth Lleuog, before reaching St Davids Head. Caves can be seen among the cliffs surrounding the promontory.

FISHGUARD *right and below*

Also known by its Welsh name, Abergwaun (mouth of the river Gwaun), Fishguard is located in northern Pembrokeshire. A ferry from Goodwick harbour, a mile south of the town, travels to Rosslare in Ireland. Lower Fishguard has a pleasant quay surrounded by cottages and was used as a film location for *Moby Dick* and *Under Milk Wood*. The town has an old fort on Castle Point and was also the site of an invasion by the French in 1797. The invasion was unsuccessful and the terms of surrender following "the last invasion of Britain" were signed at the Royal Oak pub, now a lively venue in Market Square.

CARDIGAN *right and below*

Sited on the banks of the Teifi at the end of the estuary leading out into Cardigan Bay, the thriving market town of Cardigan has been a seaport since the middle ages. The long, sheltered harbour meant that the town was an ideal base for both the export of local farm produce and slate to Ireland and as a port for the herring industry. Later Cardigan became an important shipbuilding centre and the town's prosperity grew. Gradually, its fortunes as a commercial centre dwindled as the harbour silted up and large vessels were unable to enter the port.

Today Cardigan is a thriving tourist centre and contains attractive Georgian and Victorian houses, alongside traditional shops and inns. Local beaches and headlands command panoramic views over the bay. The town has a strong Welsh-speaking community and its Norman castle was the site of the first national Eisteddfod in 1176. The castle, now a ruin, is the subject of a local campaign of restoration.

ABERYSTWYTH

One of the largest towns of west Wales, Aberystwyth lies south of Snowdonia on Cardigan Bay. The harbour and marina can be seen to the south side of the town. Aberystwyth is home to the National Library of Wales (below) and one of the colleges of the University of Wales. The town's two beaches are divided by a headland on which the ruined gatehouse of Edward I's Aberystwyth Castle stands. The castle decayed rapidly due to its proximity to the Irish Sea. To protect other buildings on the shore, a wide promenade was constructed, one of the longest in Britain. Along the seafront stand brightly-painted four or five-storey Victorian buildings, many used as hotels or guesthouses, and a few homes for the town's sizeable student population. Situated on the north shore is the grand Old College Building, bought in 1872 to establish the University College of Wales. It was originally designed by John Nash to become the luxury Castle Hotel, but went bankrupt before completion. Stunning views of Cardigan Bay can be seen from the hills surrounding the town. On a clear day, it is possible to see the peak of Snowdon, 50 miles to the north.

ABERDOVEY

The peaceful seaside village of Aberdovey, also known as Aberdyfi, is situated on the north side of the entrance to the Dyfi estuary. It has a picturesque setting in the midst of steep green hills in an area of sheep farms. Founded around shipbuilding, the village is today popular with holidaymakers. The resort has a large number of holiday homes and attractions include yachting, fishing and golf. The extensive sands are clean and popular with families in the summer; brightly-painted buildings along the beachfront add to the holiday atmosphere.

MACHYNLLETH *below right*

Known locally as Mach, this small market town has an ancient history. Situated 10 miles inland from Cardigan Bay on the river Dyfi, the town is the site of Owain Glyndwr's Welsh parliament of 1404. Now a museum, the building is open to the public in the summer months. Machynlleth is also known for its prominent clock tower which was built in the late 19th century and is nearly 80ft (24m) tall. The town contains medieval and Victorian architecture, and is also home to MOMA, the Welsh Museum of Modern Art. Agriculture is still an important industry and there is increasing employment in the renewable energy industry.

BORTH *above*

With one of the longest beaches in Ceredigion at over three miles long,
it is not surprising that Borth, about seven miles north of Aberystwyth,
is a popular tourist destination. The beach has golden sands at low tide and a
shingle shore at high tide. Borth started life as a fishing village with a thriving
herring industry but the arrival of the railways in the 1860s brought visitors to
the seashore. A number of Victorian hotels sprang up, many of which still
stand. Popular with surfers, Borth also has an Animalarium which houses a
collection of interesting and unusual animals.

THE DOVEY

The river Dovey or Afon Dyfi flows from close by the mountain Aran Fawddwy through Machynlleth to the sea at Aberdyfi. It forms a natural boundary between north and south Wales and is a dramatic region of saltmarshes, mudflats and sandbanks. Frequent flooding occurs and some roads in the lower sections can become impassable. In the saltmarshes quicksand can also be a hazard. The estuary is home to the Dyfi National Nature Reserve, and many birds such as oystercatchers, curlews and cormorants. The reserve was founded in 1958 to protect the region from the pressures of tourism and the impact of modern farming methods. Today the river is free from pollutants and notable for its salmon and brown trout. The Dyfi valley (below) which lies on the southern rim of Snowdonia is the natural border between north and south Wales and is famous for its natural beauty. From here there are stunning views of Cadair Idris to the north and easy access to the Aran mountains at the head of the valley.

CENTRE FOR ALTERNATIVE TECHNOLOGY *left*

Situated close to Machynlleth, the Centre for Alternative Technology offers practical solutions to environmental problems. It contains a visitor centre where it is possible to find out about renewable energy and ways to tackle climate change, pollution and the waste of precious resources. A small community lives at the centre, putting into practice cooperative and environmental ideas. Exhibits include a water-balanced funicular railway, a low-energy house and solar, hydro and wind power.

SEVERN CROSSING

The original Severn Bridge (left) is today an icon of Wales, forming the southern gateway from England. Its opening in 1966 by the Queen was hailed as the start of a new era of economic expansion in south Wales. Until then, the Severn Estuary was crossed by ferry between Aust in south Gloucestershire and Beachley in Monmouthshire. The Severn Bridge (Pont Hafren) was built, connecting the M4 to Wales. It followed almost the exact route of the old ferry crossing. High winds and increasing traffic on the suspension bridge led to demand for a second crossing, which was constructed five miles downstream in 1996. Known as the Second Severn Bridge it carries the M4 traffic, making the original Severn Bridge a lesser-used route into Wales. The beauty and grace of the original bridge is such that it was listed in 1998.